CW00517024

The Keto Diet Cookbook for Beginners 2019

The Comprehensive Guide to Ketogenic Diet to Improve

Your Health, Heal Your Body and Living Keto Lifestyle

By Marla Cook

Legal & Disclaimer s

The information and contents herein are not designed to replace or take the place of any form of medical or professional advice and are not meant to replace the need for independent medical, financial, legal or other professional advice or services, as may be required. The content and information in this book have been provided for educational and entertainment purposes only.

The content and information in this book have been compiled from reliable sources and are accurate to the author's best knowledge, information, and belief. The author cannot guarantee this book's accuracy and validity and cannot be held liable for any errors and/or omissions. Further, changes will be periodically made to this book when needed. It is recommended that you consult with a health professional who is familiar with your personal medical history before using any of the suggested remedies, techniques, or information in this book.

Table of Content

Introduction

I hope you'll agree with me at this point that the Ketogenic diet is one of the simplest menus around. To follow the Ketogenic diet, you just need to do one thing: eat high-fat, moderate protein, and low carb. Eating a high-fat diet leads your body into a state called Ketosis. In Ketosis, your body will burn fat for energy, leading to incredible weight loss benefits.

Everyone has a different body, so you'll need to pay attention to the signs and listen to your body to determine when you're in Ketosis. In general, your body can reach Ketosis very quickly. Ideally, if you commit to the diet and don't snack on carbs, you should enter Ketosis within one or two days.

The fastest way to enter Ketosis is by fasting. By not eating anything with caloric value for a 24-hour period, the body will begin Ketosis to find enough energy. If you break your fast with a high-fat, low carbohydrate meal, you will be able to keep your body in Ketosis going forward.

Alternatively, begin eating the high-fat, low carbohydrate Ketogenic diet, and after two or three days, your body should be in Ketosis.

Chapter1 All About Keto Diet

What is a Ketogenic Diet?

The ketogenic diet, broadly defined, is a high-fat, medium-protein, low-carbohydrate diet. A ketogenic diet helps the body produce ketones, which help fat replace carbohydrates to provide energy to the body and promote fat consumption. Ketogenic diets, low-carb diets, and low-carb high-fat (LCHF) diets all refer to different approaches to ketogenic diets.

How the Ketogenic Diet Works

Our bodies are more attuned to converting glucose with ease for use as energy. When you eat something high in carbohydrates (carbs), your body will produce glucose and insulin. The hormone, Insulin, has the ability to process the glucose or sugar in your bloodstream by taking it around the body. Since glucose is being used as the body's primary energy source, fats are rendered redundant and they accumulated in the body. Now, on a regular carbohydrate diet, our bodies are designed to look to glucose for energy. But you can change all that by lowering carbs and putting fats to good use. Fats are processed into ketones for use as an energy source when the intake of carbs are lowered. In other words, that redundant fat that is responsible for excessive weight can be burnt for energy just by eliminating regular carbs from diet. This translates to unprecedented weight loss on the part of the practitioner. The production of ketones from fats in the liver is known as ketogenesis; hence, the diet's name.

What is Ketosis?

This is the state the body is put into when you progressively eliminate carbs from diet. It is the body's own survival mechanism when food intake becomes low. Ketosis provokes the production of ketones from the breakdown of fats in the liver. A keto diet endgame is to trick your body into this metabolic state. And this is not achieved via outright starvation but via carbohydrate starvation.

It will amaze you just how adept our bodies are at adapting to what you stuff it with. When you stuff it with fats and starve it of carbohydrates, it will begin to burn fats into ketones as its

primary energy source. As earlier illustrated, weight loss, controlled blood sugar, increased mental focus, increased energy, controlled appetite, optimal blood pressure and improved good cholesterol levels are some of the amazing features of optimum ketone levels,

How to Reach Ketosis

Sounds easy, doesn't it? Achieving ketosis, I mean. But it's easy to get bamboozled with all the information that is available out there. According to their degrees of importance, here are some things you should consider making your mantra.

Keep your Carbohydrates in Check: Don't just focus on net carbs. For best results, keep your net carbs below 20g and your total carbs below 35g per day.

Restrict Your Protein Intake: Especially for those coming into keto from an Atkins diet who are unlikely to have been moderate with proteins, you need to watch it. Too much protein can disrupt ketosis. For successful weight loss, keep proteins between 0.6 and 0.8g per pound lean body mass.

Don't Worry About Fats: They form the primary energy source on keto – so ensure you're getting good amounts of it. Weight loss on keto isn't hinged on starvation.

Drink Plenty of Water: Stay hydrated with sufficient water intake. Drink water constantly for its aids the regulation of several vital bodily functions and also helps to control hunger levels.

Quit Snacking: You stand a better chance of losing weight with keto when you have fewer insulin spikes during the day. Indiscriminate and incessant snacking could stall or slow down weight loss which will do your chances of succeeding with the keto weight loss program no good.

Start Fasting: This doesn't imply outright starvation. All you really need to do is to cut down on your consumption. Fasting is a proven way to up ketone levels. This part is very essential to the weight loss program

Add Some Exercise Too: Light workout sessions will certainly do no wrong. There is nothing as healthy as some good old-fashioned walk in the park or 20-30 minutes sessions on the treadmill. You are sure going to get the most out of your ketogenic diet when you add some exercise to your schedule.

Think About Supplementing: Though it isn't set in stone, adding some supplements to your daily diet can help up the ante. Supplements on a ketogenic diet include: MCT oil, minerals, caffeine, exogenous ketones and creatine. Keep an eye out for product labels too; you want to make sure those ingredients contained in those products are not going to set you back on your journey to health and wellbeing. It's quite common to find carbs tucked away in products that claim to be keto friendly.

Optimal Ketosis and Macros

There is an abundance of shortcuts, tricks and gimmicks out there that are acclaimed to be instrumental to achieving optimal ketosis – but I'd strongly recommend that you pay no mind to any of that. Make no mistake about it; dietary nutrition is the only way to accomplish optimal ketosis. Pay attention to 'only'. In everyday terms, dietary nutrition implies 'just eating food'. You can achieve optimal ketosis only by eating just the right foods in the right amounts. And you need not some magic pill to pull it off. All it takes is some dietary discipline on your part; you have got to stay strict and remain vigilant and watchful of what goes into your mouth and down your gut. You should able to account for every single calorie consumed from the off.

What You Should Eat

Not in any way like fasting, the ketogenic thin down urges you to eat. Regardless, you can't just eat any sustenance. In a keto thing down, you should merely eat new livelihoods that are low in carbs, attractive in protein, and high in fats.

Meats

Stick to meats that have an ideal measure of protein and low carb substance, for instance, ground sirloin sandwich, point, eggs, et cetera. Eat wild-got point and avoid developed fish.

Vegetables

Eat verdant greens like turnips, collards, spinach, and kale. You can in like manner eat over the ground vegetables, for instance, broccoli, squash, cauliflower, and zucchini.

High-fat dairy

High-fat sustenances are a standard bit of a ketone eat less. Fat furthermore impacts you to feel full for a more expanded period. Delineations: high fat cream, margarine, and unusual cheeses.

Nuts and seeds

Nuts and seeds are squeezed with supplements that can empower your body to stay thin and sound. Cases: macadamias, almonds, walnuts, and sunflower seeds.

Avocado and berries

Sweeteners

Use sweeteners that have the most negligible count of sugars, for instance, Splenda, stevia, cleric essential item, Sweet n Low, et cetera.

Distinctive fats

Other incredible wellsprings of fats that you can unite into your keto refrain from sustenance are a high-fat serving of blended greens dressing, coconut oil, and drenched fans.

Keep in mind that keto abstains from food is deficient in starches, coordinate in protein, and high in fat. A typical ketone eating regimen may be addressed as takes after:

Fats – 70% Protein – 25% Carbohydrates – 5%

It is proposed to take between 20-30g of net carbs consistently for a ketone expend fewer calories. Regardless, if you have to hit ketosis quickly, you may consider fewer carbs and keep your glucose levels low. In case getting more fit is your inspiration of doing a keto devour fewer calories, by then it is decidedly recommended that you watch your total sugars and net starches. When you participate in a ketone eating routine and get yourself hungry, you can check your yearning by eating nuts, nutty spread, cheddar, and seeds. Do whatever it takes not to perplex your need to eat with the need to eat.

Broccoli

Broccoli is outstandingly regular on a ketone thin down. It is loaded down with vitamins C and K, and what is more, a measure of broccoli just contains 4g net carbs. Distinctive examinations in like manner show that the people who have sort two diabetes can benefit by eating broccoli since it cuts down insulin resistance. Broccoli can result in like manner shield you from a couple of types of development. Everything thought of it as is a staple support in a ketone tally calories and is to a significant degree accommodating.

Asparagus

Asparagus is loaded down with vitamins C, A, and K. Thinks furthermore exhibit that it can help reduce strain and secure personality prosperity.

Creatures

If you are exhausted on debilitating dishes, just incorporate a couple of mushrooms and value a delightful dinner. For cases, combining tyke tolls in a mushroom cauliflower risotto will give it better surface and flavor. Youngster Bellas are in like manner low in carbs, at only 1g net carb per glass.

Mushrooms

Mushrooms have exceptional alleviating properties. An examination shows that the people who metabolic turmoil have seen fundamental redesigns inside four months.

Squash

Many types of squash have high sugar, and you should ensure that you pick the correct squash for your eating regimen. The best and most used is the mid-year squash. Summer squash is now and then utilized as a noodle substitution in dishes. It is high in fat and a marvelous side dish to oblige your meal

Spinach

Spinach contains vitamins and minerals. Additionally, it is heart friendly and reduces eye pains.

Avocado

It is high in fat, which makes it one of the best food for a fat supplement. It is rich in vitamin C and potassium.

Cauliflower

Known as the star of dishes, cauliflower is a versatile setting that can be added to different kind of dinners. It can be used for pizzas, wraps, suppers, and pureed potatoes. With only 2g net sugars for each glass, it is not surprising that cauliflower is a champion among the most consistently used fixings in some low-starch diets.

Green beans

Joined into the vegetable family, greens beans have fewer carbs than various conventional items. They are on occasion called as snap peas. A measure of green beans just contains 6g net carbs, which makes them a splendid development to any devour.

Kale and lettuce

Used as a piece of servings of blended greens far and wide, kale and lettuce are a not too bad low-sugar elective. They are moreover a beautiful wellspring of vitamins A and C and can help cut down the threats of heart infections.

Regardless of the way that kale is more nutritious than lettuce, it furthermore has more carbs per serving. Consequently, be wary how much kale you eat up in light of the way that sugars can incorporate speedily.

Do Not Eat

Grains and Starches

Swear off eating wheat-based product, rice, pasta, cereal and oats.

High Sugar Foods

Cake, juice, ice cream, candy, sweets, nectar, maple syrup, even dark-hued sugar and so on.

Starchy Veggies

Corn, yams, potatoes, beets, carrot etc.

Most Fruits

Keep up a vital separation from or potentially control your use of essential things like bananas, apples, melons, etc.

Legumes:

Peas, Kidney beans, lentils, chickpeas etc.

Dieting Principles

Doing the ketogenic diet requires adhering to some principles which include the following:

- 60-75% of your daily calories should come from fat, 15-30% from protein and only 5-10% should come from carbohydrates.

- Your daily net carbs consumption should be less than 50 grams. Daily Net carbs are calculated by deducting fiber contents from sugar contents.

- While it helps to keep an eye on your calorie intake, you should never ignore your body needs.

- Eat moderate amounts of proteins. You can use your body fat percentage to determine the most appropriate amount of protein you should be taking daily. You should choose between 0.6 and 1 gram per pound of lean body mass.

- Let most of your calories from fat come from the standard types of fat like the monounsaturated fats, saturated fats, and omega 3s.

- If your net carb limit is low, you should avoid fruits and other low carb treats.

- Don't starve yourself. Ensure that you eat whenever you are hungry.

- Shop weekly and get rid of anything that is not allowed on a diet from your home.

- Avoid processed foods as some of the time may contain hidden carbs like sorbitol, maltitol, preservatives, additives and artificial sweeteners. Better still, keep your eyes on the label.

- Avoid processed fats like vegetable oils, wholly and partially hydrogenated oils, margarine, trans fats, soybean oil, corn oil and canola oil.

- Make sure you always plan your diet to avoid temptations and spontaneous eating.

4 Biggest Keto Mistakes to Avoid

Don't dirty keto

"Dirty keto is a pithy way of referring to the 'fast and dirty' practice of using premade, packaged foods instead of homemade food crafted from whole food ingredients," - Stephanie Pedersen.

"Go vegetable heavy. Reverse the psychology of your plate by making meat the side dish and vegetables the main course." —Bobby Flay

Both quotes tell us of how Grandma advised us to eat, and it is quite surprising that the keto diet follows the same principles. In everything that you do, make sure to eat your highly fats foods in the healthiest forms, and the same applies to all other ingredients. Go for organic, non-GMO, and grass-fed options because they are not chemically modified.

Eat moderate proteins always

Do not believe the lie that proteins make you lose weight; they do not. Excessive proteins tend to increase insulin levels, which in turn will increase weight.

For bodybuilders, a little extra protein may be essential for building muscles, but this should be matched against the Standard Ketogenic Diet type. You still ought to be ketosis.

Don't swap water and sleep for anything else

"The human body is a miraculous self-healing machine, but those self-repair systems require a nutrient-dense diet." —Joel Fuhrman

A nutrient-dense diet includes a good drink of water daily. And as the body goes through its new development for the keto diet, taking enough rest at night and during the day is necessary to keep the body energetic, satiated, and happy. Do not for a second, ever compromise on water and sleep.

Don't walk the lifestyle alone

Support systems are the best ways for growth because they watch your back and correct your trail. I find family, close friends, medical professionals, work colleagues, and a certified keto community to be the best forms of support that we need on the keto diet.

Meanwhile, ensure that your selected group of individuals are people that will genuinely care and support you through the journey.

10 Quick Tips to Keto Success

Grab these on the go as quick reminders:

- Identify your needs, desires, and plan your keto path accordingly.
- Inform and build a support system to walk hand in hand with you through the new journey.
- Organize yourself; your eating patterns, budget, schedule, design, and follow with a keto meal plan.
- Cook your food, carry your lunch packs, and pre-plan eat-outs to ensure that you can eat low-carb foods wherever you go.
- Do not trade sleep and water for anything. Make them your best pals, especially in your early keto days.

- Work closely with your doctor and workout instructor so that you're living the keto life that your body needs.
- Carry keto snacks in your bags and keep them on standby for those days when you feel a hunger pang in between meals.
- Take the keto path a step at a time. Count your achievements and disappointment as progress. And you should never give up.
- Above all, make it a fun, exciting, and rewarding ride.

Chapter2 Breakfast

Sausage and Asparagus and Egg Baked Breakfast

Preparation and Cooking Time 50 minutes
Servings 6

Ingredients:

- Sausage; chopped – 1 pound
- Asparagus stalks; chopped – 6
- Eggs; whisked – 8
- Coconut oil; melted – 1 tablespoon
- Dill; chopped – 1 tablespoon
- Leek; chopped – 1
- Coconut milk, unsweetened and full-fat – 1/4 cup
- Garlic powder – 1/4tsp.
- Salt – ½tsp.
- Ground black pepper – ¼tsp.

Directions:

1. Set oven to 350 ℉ and let preheat.
2. Place a skillet pan over medium heat and when hot, add sausage and cook for 3 to 5 minutes or until nicely browned.
3. In the meantime, crack eggs in a bowl, add garlic powder and dill, season with salt and black pepper, pour in the milk and whisk well until smooth.
4. Then add leek and asparagus into the pan and cook for 3 minutes.
5. Take a baking dish, grease with oil, then pour in the egg mixture and top with sausage-veggie mixture.
6. Place baking dish into the oven and bake for 40 minutes or until cooked through.
7. Serve straightaway.

Nutrition:
Calories: 340; Fat : 12; Fiber : 3; Carbs : 8; Protein : 23

Parsley Biscuits

Preparation and Cooking Time 20 minutes

Servings 6

Ingredients:

- Coconut oil – 6 tablespoons
- Coconut flour – 6 tablespoons
- Minced garlic – 1tsp.
- Minced white onion – 1/4 cup
- Apple cider vinegar – 1/2tsp.
- Baking soda – 1/4tsp.
- Chopped parsley – 1 tablespoon
- Coconut milk, unsweetened – 2 tablespoons
- Eggs – 2
- Salt – ½tsp.
- Ground black pepper – ¼tsp.

Directions:

1. Set oven to 350 ℉ and let preheat.
2. Crack eggs into a bowl, add flour along with remaining ingredients except for vinegar and soda and stir well until combined.
3. Stir together soda and vinegar in a bowl until mixed, then add to the prepared batter and stir until mixed.
4. Drop spoonful of the prepared batter on baking sheets lined with parchment paper and spread into a circle.
5. Place the baking sheet into the oven and bake for 15 minutes or until biscuits are nicely golden brown.
6. Serve straightaway.

Nutrition:

Calories: 140; Fat : 6; Fiber : 2; Carbs : 10; Protein : 12

Tomato and Serrano Pepper Shakshouka

Preparation and Cooking Time 30 minutes

Servings 4

Ingredients:

- Tomatoes; chopped – 3
- Minced garlic – 1 ½tsp.
- Ghee – 1 tablespoon
- Red chili powder – 1/4tsp.
- Chopped cilantro – 1 tablespoon
- Eggs – 6
- Medium white onion, peeled and chopped – 1
- Red bell pepper; chopped – 1
- Paprika – 1tsp.
- Cumin – 1tsp.
- Serrano pepper; chopped – 1
- Salt – ½tsp.
- Ground black pepper – ¼tsp.

Directions:

1. Place a skillet pan over medium heat, add ghee and when it melts, add onion and cook for 10 minutes.
2. Then add garlic and Serrano pepper and cook for 1 minute or until fragrant.
3. Add red bell pepper, stir and continue cooking for 10 minutes.
4. Add remaining ingredients except for eggs and cilantro, stir well and cook for 10 minutes.
5. Then crack eggs into the pan, season with salt and black pepper to taste and cook for 6 minutes or more until eggs are cooked to the desired level, covering the pan.
6. Sprinkle cilantro over eggs and serve.

Nutrition:

Calories: 300; Fat : 12; Fiber : 3. 4; Carbs : 22; Protein : 14

Bacon and Lemon Thyme Muffins

Preparation and Cooking Time 35 minutes

Servings 12

Ingredients:

- Bacon; finely chopped – 1 cup
- Baking soda – 1tsp.
- Eggs – 4
- Ghee, melted – 1/2 cup
- Almond flour – 3 cups
- Lemon thyme – 2tsps.
- Salt – ½tsp.
- Ground black pepper – ¼tsp.

Directions:

1. Set oven to 350 °F and let preheat.
2. Place flour in a bowl, add egg and baking soda and whisk well until incorporated.
3. Add bacon, season with salt and black pepper, then add lemon thyme and ghee and stir until well combined.
4. Take a muffin tray with 12 cups, grease with oil, then distribute the batter in them and place into the oven to bake for 20 minutes.
5. When done, remove muffin tray from the oven, cool for 10 minutes, then take out muffins and serve.

Nutrition:

Calories: 213; Fat : 7; Fiber : 2; Carbs : 9; Protein : 8

Bacon and Avocado Muffins

Preparation and Cooking Time 40 minutes

Servings 12

Ingredients:

- Slices of bacon; chopped – 6
- Chopped white onion – 1
- Baking soda – 1/2tsp.
- Coconut flour – 1/2 cup
- Coconut milk, unsweetened and full-fat – 1 cup
- Chopped avocado – 2 cups
- Eggs – 4
- Salt – ½tsp.
- Ground black pepper – ¼tsp.

Directions:

1. Set oven to 350 °F and let preheat.
2. In the meantime, place a skillet pan over medium heat and when hot, add bacon and onion and cook for 3 to 5 minutes or until nicely golden brown.
3. In the meantime, place the avocado in a bowl, mash with a fork, then add eggs and continue mashing the mixture until smooth.
4. Add flour and baking soda, season with salt and black pepper, pour in the milk and stir until well combined.
5. When bacon mixture is cooked, add it into the egg mixture and stir well.
6. Take a 12-cups muffin tray, grease with oil, then evenly distribute muffin batter in them and place into the oven to bake for 20 minutes or until muffins are set, and the top is nicely golden brown.
7. When done, let muffins cool for 10 minutes, then take them out and serve.

Nutrition:

Calories: 200; Fat : 7; Fiber : 4; Carbs : 7; Protein : 5

Radish and Corned Beef Hash

Preparation and Cooking Time 15 minutes

Servings 2

Ingredients:

- Corned beef; chopped – 2 cups
- Radishes; cut in quarters – 1 pound
- Chopped white onion – 1
- Beef stock – 1/2 cup
- Coconut oil – 1 tablespoon
- Minced garlic – ½tsp.
- Salt – ½tsp.
- Ground black pepper – ¼tsp.

Directions:

1. Place a skillet pan over medium-high heat, add oil and when hot, add onion and cook for 4 minutes.
2. Then add radish, stir and continue cooking for 5 minutes.
3. Stir in garlic and cook for 1 minute or until fragrant, then add remaining ingredients and stir until mixed.
4. Continue cooking hash for 5 minutes, then remove the pan from heat and serve.

Nutrition:

Calories: 240; Fat : 7; Fiber : 3; Carbs : 12; Protein : 8

Soft Cinnamon Pancakes

Preparation and Cooking Time 20 minutes

Servings 4

Ingredients:

- Cream cheese – 2 ounces
- Stevia – 1tsp.
- Ground cinnamon – 1/2tsp.
- Eggs – 2

Directions:

1. Crack eggs in a bowl, add remaining ingredients and whisk using an electric blender until smooth.
2. Place a skillet pan over medium-high heat, grease with oil and when hot, pour in a ¼ portion of batter, spread into a thin circle and cook for 2 minutes per side until cooked through and nicely golden brown.
3. Use remaining batter to cook more pancakes in the same manner and serve.

Nutrition:

Calories: 344; Fat : 23; Fiber : 12; Carbs : 3; Protein : 16

Flax, Chia, and Pumpkin Pancakes

Preparation and Cooking Time 40 minutes

Servings 6

Ingredients:

- Hazelnut flour – 2 ounces
- Ground flax seeds – 2 ounces
- Egg white protein – 1 ounce
- Coconut oil – 1tsp.
- Chai masala – 1 tablespoon
- Vanilla extract, unsweetened – 1tsp.
- Baking powder – 1tsp.
- Coconut cream – 1 cup
- Swerve sweetener – 1 tablespoon
- Pumpkin puree – 1/2 cup
- Eggs – 3
- Drops of stevia – 5

Directions:

1. Crack eggs in a bowl, add sweetener, stevia, vanilla, pumpkin puree, and coconut cream and whisk well until smooth.
2. Place remaining ingredients in another bowl and stir until mixed.
3. Add egg mixture into the flour mixture and stir well until incorporated.
4. Place a skillet pan over medium-high heat, grease with oil and when hot, pour in 1/6 of the mixture and spread in a circle.
5. Cook for 3 minutes per side or until cooked through and nicely golden brown and transfer to a plate.
6. Use remaining batter to cook more pancakes in the same manner and serve straight away.

Nutrition:

Calories: 400; Fat : 23; Fiber : 4; Carbs : 5; Protein : 21

Brussels Sprouts with Eggs and Bacon

Preparation and Cooking Time 25 minutes

Servings 3

Ingredients:

- Brussels sprouts, sliced – 12 ounces
- Bacon; chopped – 2 ounces
- Shallots, minced – 2
- Minced garlic – 1tsp.
- Apple cider vinegar – 1½ tablespoons
- Eggs – 3
- Ghee; melted – 1 tablespoon
- Salt – ½tsp.
- Ground black pepper – ¼tsp.

Directions:

1. Place a skillet pan over medium heat and when hot, add bacon and cook for 3 to 5 minutes or until crispy.
2. When done, transfer bacon to a plate and set aside until required.
3. Add sprouts into the pan, season with salt and black pepper, then drizzle with vinegar, stir well and cook for 5 minutes.
4. Then return bacon into the pan, stir and continue cooking for 5 minutes.
5. Stir in ghee, then create three wells in the center of the pan and crack an egg in it.
6. Cook egg for 3 to 5 minutes or until cooked to the desired level, then remove the pan from heat and serve straight away.

Nutrition:

Calories: 240; Fat : 7; Fiber : 4; Carbs : 7; Protein : 12

Hemp, Flax and Chia Seeds Porridge

Preparation and Cooking Time 5 minutes

Servings 1

Ingredients:

- Chia seeds – 1 tablespoon
- Hemp hearts – 1/2 cup and 1 tablespoon
- Ground cinnamon – 1/2tsp.
- Stevia – 1 tablespoon
- Almond milk – 1 cup
- Flax seeds – 2 tablespoons
- Almond flour – 1/4 cup
- Vanilla extract, unsweetened – 3/4tsp.

Directions:

1. Place a ½ cup of hemp hearts into a medium saucepan, add chia and flax seeds along with stevia, cinnamon, vanilla, and almond milk and stir well.
2. Place saucepan over medium heat and cook for 2 minutes.
3. Then remove the saucepan from heat, stir in almond flour and then transfer the mixture into a bowl.
4. Top porridge with remaining hemp hearts and serve.

Nutrition:

Calories: 230; Fat : 12; Fiber : 7; Carbs : 3; Protein : 43

Tea Flavored Eggs

Preparation and Cooking Time 4 hours and 15 minutes

Servings 12

Ingredients:

- Tamari sauce – 1 cup
- Star anise – 6
- Tea bags – 4
- Ground black pepper – 1tsp.
- Whole peppercorns – 1 tablespoon
- Water – 8 cups
- Eggs – 12
- Ground cinnamon – 2 tablespoons
- Salt – 4 tablespoons

Directions:

1. Place a large pot over medium heat half full with water, bring water to boil, then add eggs and cook for 5 to 7 minutes or until hard boiled.
2. When done, transfer eggs into a bowl containing chilled water, let cool completely, then crack them, don't peel the eggs.
3. Drain pot, then pour in water, add remaining ingredients and stir until mixed.
4. Place pot over low heat, bring to simmer, then add peeled eggs and cook for 30 minutes, covering the pot.
5. Then remove and discard tea bags and cook eggs for 3 hours and 30 minutes.
6. When done, cool eggs at room temperature, peel them and serve.

Nutrition:

Calories: 90; Fat : 6; Fiber : 0; Carbs : 0; Protein : 7

Beef, Olives, Avocado and Egg Breakfast Bowl

Preparation and Cooking Time 25 minutes

Servings 1

Ingredients:

- Ground beef – 4 ounces
- Sliced mushrooms – 8
- Medium white onion, peeled and chopped – 1
- Smoked paprika – 1/2 tsp.
- Black olives; pitted and sliced – 12
- Eggs, whisked – 2
- Avocado; pitted, peeled and chopped – 1
- Coconut oil – 1 tablespoon
- Salt – ¾tsp.
- Ground black pepper – 1/4tsp.

Directions:

1. Place a skillet pan over medium heat, add oil and when hot, add onion and mushrooms.
2. Season onion and mushrooms with salt and black pepper and cook for 5 minutes.
3. Then add beef, season with paprika, stir well and cook for 10 minutes or until cooked through.
4. Transfer beef mixture into a bowl and set aside until required.
5. Return pan over medium heat, grease with oil, then add whisked eggs, season with remaining salt and black pepper and cook for 3 minutes or more until eggs are scrambled.
6. Return beef mixture into the pan, stir well, then add avocado and olives and continue cooking for 1 minute or until heated through.
7. Transfer beef-egg mixture into a bowl and serve.

Nutrition:

Calories: 600; Fat : 23; Fiber : 8; Carbs : 22; Protein : 43

Creamy Feta Cheese Omelet

Total Time: 20 minutes

Serves: 1

Ingredients:

- Jarred pesto, 1 tbsp.
- Heavy cream, 1 tbsp.
- Salt
- Ghee, 1 tbsp.
- Crumbled feta cheese, 1 oz.
- Black pepper
- Eggs, 3.

Directions:

1. Using a medium bowl, add in pepper, heavy cream and eggs. Mix thoroughly until well combined.
2. Set a pan over medium heat. Add ghee and warm. Pour in the above mixture in step 1. Cook well until the omelet becomes fluffy.
3. Sprinkle the omelet with pesto and cheese, fold them in halves and cook for 5 more minutes while covered
4. Set the omelet on a serving platter and enjoy.

Nutrition:

calories: 500, protein: 30, carbs: 3, fat: 43, fiber: 6

Chia and Coconut Pudding

Total Time: 40 minutes

Serves: 2

Ingredients:

- Coffee, 2 tbsps.
- Cocoa nibs, 2 tbsps.
- Chia seeds, 1/3 cup
- Water, 2 cup
- Swerve, 1 tbsp.
- Coconut cream, 1/3 cup
- Vanilla extract, 1 tbsp.

Directions:

1. Set a pot over medium high heat. Add in water and heat to boil. Add in coffee and allow to simmer for about 15 minutes. Kill the heat and ensure to strain the mixture into a clean bowl.
2. In the bowl, stir in the remaining ingredients. Refrigerate for half an hour.
3. Divide amongst 2 bowls and enjoy.

Nutrition:

calories: 100, protein: 3, fat: 0.4, carbs: 3, fiber: 4

Chapter3 Lunch

Chicken & Garnished Shrimp

Total Time: 30 minutes

Serves: 2

Ingredients:

- Lime juice, 2 tsps.
- Spinach leaves, 2 handfuls.
- Xanthan gum, ¼ tsp.
- Salt.
- Garlic powder, 1 tsp.
- Coconut oil, 1 tbsp.
- Raw de veined shrimp, 20.
- Crushed red pepper, ½ tsp.
- Roughly chopped mushrooms, ½ lb.
- Chopped green onion stalk, 1.
- De-boned chicken breasts, 2.
- Black pepper.
- Mayonnaise, ¼ cup
- Sriracha, 2 tbsps.
- Paprika, ½ tsp.

Directions:

1. Set a pan over medium heat. Add in oil and heat. Add in chicken breasts seasoned with the peppers, salt, and garlic powder. Allow 8 minutes of cooking before flipping to cook the other side for 6 more minutes.

2. Add in mushrooms and cook for some minutes. Add in more pepper and salt if desired.

3. Set a separate pan over a medium source of heat. Stir in xanthan, shrimp, mayo, paprika and sriracha and cook for some minutes until the shrimp becomes pink.

4. Remove from heat and stir in lime juice.

5. Split the spinach amongst the serving bowls. Do the same with the chicken and mushroom using the same bowls. Apply a topping of shrimp mixture and a garnish of green onions. Enjoy the meal.

Nutrition:

calories: 500, fiber: 10, fat: 34, carbs: 3, protein: 40

Zucchini Noodles and Bacon Salad

Total Time: 10 minutes

Serves: 2

Ingredients:

- Crumbled blue cheese, 1/3 cup
- Black pepper.
- Zucchini noodles, 4 cup
- Cooked and crumbled bacon, 1/2 cup
- Baby spinach, 1 cup
- Thick cheese dressing, 1/3 cup

Directions:

1. Combine spinach with bacon, zucchini noodles, and blue cheese in a salad bowl.
2. Toss in cheese dressing and black pepper as required to coat evenly.
3. Set into 2 bowls then serve

Nutrition:

calories: 200, fat: 14, fiber: 4, carbs: 2, protein: 10

Pan-Fried Crab Cakes

Total Time: 22 minutes

Serves: 6

Ingredients:

- Old bay seasoning, 1 tsp.
- Lemon juice, 1 tsp.
- Mayonnaise, ½ cup
- Chopped parsley, ¼ cup
- Egg, 1.
- Crab meat, 1 lb.
- Minced jalapeno pepper, 1 tsp.
- Black pepper.
- Mustard powder, ½ tsp.
- Chopped green onions, 2.
- Worcestershire sauce, 1 tsp.
- Salt
- Chopped cilantro, ¼ cup
- Olive oil, 2 tbsps.

Directions:

1. Combine the seasonings, crab meat, cilantro, parsley, green onions, lemon juice, jalapeno, mustard powder, old bay seasoning, and Worcestershire sauce in a mixing bowl.
2. Whisk mayo and eggs in another bowl
3. Combine the two mixtures. Mold the mixture into 6 patties then set them on a plate.
4. Set the pan with oil on fire to melt for frying the crab cakes for 3 minutes on both sides over medium heat then set on a paper towels.
5. Repeat the process with the remaining cakes and serve.

Nutrition:

calories: 254, fat: 17, fiber: 1, carbs: 1, protein: 20

Spicy beef sauerkraut soup bowls

Preparation and cooking time: 1 hour 30 minutes

Serves: 8

Ingredients:

- Beef stock- 14 oz.
- Chopped parsley- 3 tbsp.
- Ground beef- 1 Ib.
- Chopped sauerkraut- 14 oz.
- Chicken stock- 2 cups
- Canned tomatoes and juice- 14 oz.
- Olive oil- 3 tsp.
- Minced garlic- 1 tbsp.
- Water- 2 cups
- Dried sage- 1 tsp.
- Gluten-free Worcestershire sauce- 1 tbsp.
- Ste via- 1 tbsp.
- Bay leaves- 4
- Chopped onion- 1
- Salt
- Pepper

Directions

1. Brown beef on both sides in a pan with oil for 10 minutes.
2. Mix stock, tomatoes, Worcestershire sauce, sauerkraut, parsley, bay leaf and sage in a pot and let boil slowly under medium heat.
3. Add the beef and let it continue to cook.
4. Pour the remaining oil in a pan and add the onions to cook for 2 minutes then add the garlic and cook for 1 minute.
5. Add the garlic and onion mix to the soup pot and let it cook for 1 hour.
6. Mix in salt, pepper and add water. Cook for 15 minutes.
7. Serve into bowls.

Nutrition:

Calories 250, carbs 3, protein 12, fiber 1, fat 5

Spicy beef soup

Preparation and cooking time: 8 hours 10 minutes

Serves: 4

Ingredients:

- Ground beef- 2½ Ib.
- Chopped pickled jalapeños- ½ cup
- Chopped canned tomatoes and green chilies- 15 oz.
- Dried oregano- 1 tsp.
- Red onion: chopped- 1
- Bay leaf- 1
- Tomato paste- 6 oz.
- Garlic powder- 1 tsp.
- Onion powder- 1 tsp.
- Pinch of cayenne pepper
- Ground cumin- 2 tbsp.
- Coconut aminos- 2 tbsp.
- Chili powder- 4 tbsp.
- Minced garlic- 4 tbsp.
- Chopped celery ribs- 3
- Salt and black pepper

Directions:

1. Put the beef in a pan over medium-high and add the salt, pepper, half the garlic and half of the onions and cook until beef is brown.
2. Pour the beef mix in a slow cooker and add the other ingredients.
3. Let it cook on low for 8 hours.
4. Serve into bowls.

Nutrition:

Calories 137, carbs 5, protein 17, fiber 2, fat 6

Easy Turkey and Tomato Curry

The preparation and cooking time is 30 minutes and can sufficiently serve 4 people

Ingredients

- Turmeric- 1 tablespoon
- Ground Coriander- 1 tablespoon
- Chopped canned tomatoes – 20 ounces
- Ground cumin – 1 tablespoon
- Spinach – 3 ounces
- Chilli powder – 2 tablespoons
- Sliced yellow onions – 2
- Minced garlic cloves – 2
- Grated ginger – 2 tablespoons
- Coconut cream – 2 tablespoon
- Salt and black pepper
- Minced turkey meat – 18 ounces
- Chopped canned tomatoes – 20 ounces

Directions:

1. Pour the coconut oil into the pan, and place over medium heat, cook it for 6 minutes
2. Put the garlic and ginger and stir thoroughly until it's evenly mixed, simmer for additional 1 minute
3. Pour the coconut cream, mix and cook for an additional 10 minutes
4. Make use of an immersion blender and mix with turkey meat and spinach, cook for 15 minutes and serve

Nutrition:

Protein 12, Calories 240, Fiber 3, Carbs 2, Fat 4

Creamy Mushroom Chicken Recipe

The preparation and cooking time is 1 hour 20 minutes, and it can sufficiently and serve 4 people

Ingredients:

- Coconut Oil – 1 tablespoon
- Minced garlic cloves – 4
- Whipping cream – 1 cup
- Chopped Parsley – A handful
- Chopped yellow onion – 1
- Chopped bacon strips – 4
- Cremini mushrooms – 10 ounces
- Chicken thighs – 8
- White Chardonnay wine – 2 cups
- Salt and black pepper

Directions:

1. Put a pan over a medium heat
2. Add Bacon, stir and cook until it becomes crispy
3. Take it off the heat and transfer to the paper towels
4. Heat the pan with the bacon fat, put the chicken, add the salt and pepper, cook for few minutes until they get brown and transfer to the brown paper
5. Heat the pan continuously and put the onions, and cook for an additional 5 minutes, put the garlic, stir and cook for 2 minutes before transferring to the next bacon pieces
6. Return the pan and set over a medium heat, put back the Bacon, garlic, chicken and onion to the pan
7. Put the wine, stir continuously and cook for under a reduced heat for 40 minutes
8. Put the cream and Parsley, stir and cook for 12 minutes
9. Share within plates and serve

Nutrition:

Fat 10, Protein 24, Carbs 4, Calories 340, Fiber 7

Chicken Breast with Olive Tapenade

The preparation and cooking time is 20 minutes and can sufficiently serve 2 people

Ingredients

- Coconut Oil – 2 tablespoons
- Olives tapenade – ½ cup
- Crushed garlic cloves – 3
- Chicken breast cut into pieces – 1

The tapenade

- Olive oil – 2 tablespoons
- Pitted black olives – 1 cup
- Chopped Parsley – ¼ cup
- Lemon juice – 1 tablespoon
- Salt and black pepper

Directions

1. Get a food processor
2. Mix in the pepper, salt, olive, 2 tablespoons of Olive Oil, Parsley and lemon juice
3. Blend very well and get it transferred to the bowl
4. Pour coconut oil in a pan, add garlic and cook for 3 minutes
5. Put the chicken pieces and cook for 5 minutes on each side
6. Share the chicken on each plate and top it with olives tapenade

Nutrition:

Protein 20, Calories 130, Fat 12, Fiber 0, Carbs 3

Stuffed Chicken Breast Recipe

The preparation and cooking time is 25 minutes

Ingredients

- Coconut Oil – 1 tablespoon
- Soft cream cheese – 4 ounces
- Crumbled feta cheese – 3 ounces
- Minced garlic clove – 1
- Chicken breast – 3
- Salt and black pepper
- Cooked and chopped spinach – 8

Directions

1. Get a medium-size bowl, mix in the feta cheese, salt, pepper, garlic and the cream cheese
2. Put the chicken breasts on a working surface
3. Add the stuffed chicken
4. Cook for 5 minutes on each side
5. Then move everything to an oven at 450 °F and bake for 10 minutes

Nutrition:

Calories 290, Fiber 2, Protein 24, Fat 12, Carbs 4

Mustard Salmon Meatballs

Total time: 40 minutes

Servings: 4

Ingredients:

- Coconut flour, 1 tbsp.
- Egg, 1.
- Salt
- Minced garlic cloves, 2.
- Chopped chives, 1/4 cup
- Black pepper
- Dijon mustard, 2 tbsps.
- Ghee, 2 tbsps.
- De-boned and minced wild salmon, 1 lb.
- Chopped onion, 1/3 cup

For the sauce:

- Chopped chives, 2 tbsps.
- Ghee, 2 tbsps.
- Lemon juice.
- Coconut cream, 2 cup
- Lemon zest.
- Minced garlic cloves, 4.
- Dijon mustard, 2 tbsps.

Directions:

1. Set a pan on fire to melt 2 tablespoons ghee over medium heat.
2. Mix in 2 garlic cloves and onion to cook for 3 minutes then reserve in a bowl.
3. Combine coconut flour, 2 tablespoons mustard, onion, garlic, egg and seasonings in another mixing bowl.
4. Mold meatballs from the salmon mix and set on a baking tray.
5. Set an oven for 25 minutes at 325°F, allow to bake.
6. In the meantime, set up a pan on fire to melt 2 tablespoons ghee over medium heat.
7. Stir in 4 garlic cloves to cook for 1 minute.

8. Mix in 2 tablespoons Dijon mustard, coconut cream, lemon juice, chives and zest to cook for 3 minutes.

9. Remove salmon meatballs from the oven and set them into Dijon sauce to cook for 1 minute.

10. Remove from heat and set into bowls to serve.

11. Enjoy.

Nutrition:

Calories: 171, Fat: 5, Fiber: 1, Carbs: 6, Protein: 23

Pan-Fried Tuna Cakes

Total time: 20 minutes

Servings: 12

Ingredients:

- Chopped red onion ½ cup
- Cooking oil
- Eggs, 3.
- Dried dill, ½ tsp.
- Salt
- Dried parsley, 1 tsp.
- Canned tuna, 15 oz.
- Black pepper

Directions:

1. Set up a mixing bowl to combine garlic powder, parsley, onion, tuna, eggs and seasonings.

2. Set a pan on fire to heat the oil over medium heat.

3. Add tuna cakes to cook on both sides for 5 minutes.

4. Set into plates and serve.

5. Enjoy.

Nutrition:

Calories: 140, Fat: 2, Fiber: 1, Carbs: 0.6, Protein: 6

Tasty Salmon with Caper Sauce

Total time: 30 minutes

Servings: 3

Ingredients:

- Minced garlic cloves, 4.
- Lemon juice, 3 tbsps.
- Italian seasoning, 1 tbsp.
- Black pepper
- Olive oil, 1 tbsp.

- Salmon fillets, 3.
- Salt
- Capers, 2 tbsps.
- Ghee, 2 tbsps.

Directions:

1. Set a pan on fire to melt olive oil over medium heat.
2. Mix in fish fillets and season them with Italian seasoning, salt and pepper to cook for 2 minutes.
3. Turn the fish fillets to cook for 2 more minutes.
4. Remove from heat and set aside for 15 minutes to cool.
5. Set the fish to a plate and reserve.
6. Set the saucepan on fire with lemon juice, capers and garlic to cook for 2 minutes.
7. Get the pan from heat and stir in ghee.
8. Set the fish on the pan and coat evenly with sauce.
9. Set it into plates and serve.
10. Enjoy.

Nutrition:

Calories: 245, Fat: 12, Fiber: 1, Carbs: 3, Protein: 23

Tasty and Creamy Asparagus

Prep + Cook Time: 25 minutes

Servings: 3

Ingredients:

- asparagus spears - 10 ounces; cut into medium pieces and steamed
- mustard - 2 tablespoons
- cream cheese - 2 ounces
- heavy cream - 1/3 cup
- Monterey jack cheese - 1/3 cup; shredded
- Bacon - 3 tablespoons; cooked and crumbled
- Parmesan - 2 tablespoons; grated
- Salt and black pepper to the taste.

Directions:

1. Add heat to a pan containing mustard, heavy cream and cream cheese over medium heat and stir properly.
2. Add Monterey Jack cheese and parmesan; stir gently and cook until it melts
3. Add half of the bacon and the asparagus; stir gently and cook for about 3 minutes
4. Add the remaining bacon, pinch of salt and pepper to taste and stir gently. Cook for about 5 minutes
5. Divide into different plates and serve

Nutrition:

Calories: 256; Fat : 23; Fiber : 2; Carbs : 5; Protein : 13

Seasoned Sprouts Salad

Prep + Cook Time: 10 minutes

Servings: 4

Ingredients:

- alfalfa sprouts - 4 cups
- green apple - 1; cored and julienned
- dark sesame oil - 1½tsps.
- grape seed oil - 1½tsps.
- coconut milk yogurt - 1/4 cup
- nasturtium leaves - 4
- Salt and black pepper to the taste.

Directions:

1. Mix sprouts with apple and nasturtium in a salad bowl.
2. Sprinkle a pinch of salt, pepper, sesame oil, grape seed oil and coconut yogurt,
3. Toss to ensure it is well coated.
4. Divide into different plates. Serve immediately.

Nutrition:

Calories: 100; Fat : 3; Fiber : 1; Carbs : 2; Protein : 6

Avocado Salad with Cilantro

Prep + Cook Time: 10 minutes

Servings: 4

Ingredients:

- Avocados - 2; pitted and mashed
- Lime juice – 2
- white vinegar - 1 tablespoon
- coleslaw mix - 14 ounces
- olive oil - 2 tablespoons
- red onion - 1/4 cup; chopped.
- Cilantro - 1/4 cup; chopped.
- lemon stevia - 1/4tsp.
- Salt and black pepper to the taste.

Directions:

1. Put coleslaw mix in a clean salad bowl.
2. Then add avocado mash and onions, then toss to ensure it is well coated.
3. Mix lime juice with salt, pepper, oil, vinegar and stevia in a clean bowl
4. Stir gently and properly.
5. Then add this to the salad.
6. Toss to coat and sprinkle some cilantro
7. Now you can serve.

Nutrition:

Calories: 100; Fat : 10; Fiber : 2; Carbs : 5; Protein : 8

Zucchini Cream with Parmesan

Prep + Cook Time: 35 minutes

Servings: 8

Ingredients:

- Zucchinis - 6; cut in halves and then sliced
- veggie stock - 28 ounces
- oregano - 1tsp.; dried
- garlic cloves - 3; minced
- Parmesan - 2 ounces; grated
- heavy cream - 3/4 cup
- ghee - 1 tablespoon
- yellow onion - 1/2 cup; chopped.
- Salt and black pepper to the taste.

Directions:

1. Add heat to a pot containing ghee over medium high heat.
2. Then add some onions; stir gently and cook for 4 minutes
3. Add garlic; stir gently and cook for 2 more minutes.
4. Add zucchinis; stir gently and cook for another 3 minutes
5. Follow this by adding the stock; stir gently, and bring to a boil and simmer over medium heat for 15 minutes
6. Add oregano, salt and pepper before stirring gently.
7. Remove the heat and blend using an immersion blender.
8. Heat up the soup again, add heavy cream.
9. Stir gently and bring to a simmer.
10. Add parmesan; stir gently and remove the heat.
11. Ladle into different bowls
12. Serve immediately.

Nutrition:

Calories: 160; Fat : 4; Fiber : 2; Carbs : 4; Protein : 8

Arugula And Hot Broccoli Soup

Prep + Cook Time: 30 minutes

Servings: 4

Ingredients:

- broccoli head - 1; florets separated
- small yellow onion - 1; chopped.
- olive oil - 1 tablespoon
- veggie stock - 2½ cups
- clove - 1 garlic; minced
- cumin - 1tsp.; ground
- Lemon juice – ½
- arugula leaves - 1 cup
- Salt and black pepper to the taste.

Directions:

1. Heat up a pot containing oil over medium-high heat
2. Then add some onions and stir gently
3. Cook this for 4 minutes
4. Add garlic; stir and cook for another minute.
5. Add broccoli, cumin, as well as salt and pepper to taste.
6. Stir gently and cook for 4 minutes
7. Add stock; stir again and cook for extra 8 minutes
8. Use an immersion blender to blend the soup, then add half of the arugula and blend again.
9. Add the remaining arugula; stir gently and add more heat.
10. Finally add some lemon juice; stir gently.
11. Ladle into soup bowls
12. Serve immediately.

Nutrition:

Calories: 150; Fat : 3; Fiber : 1; Carbs : 3; Protein : 7

Spiced Turkey Chili

Total time: 10 minutes

Servings: 4

Ingredients:

- Sour cream, ¼ cup
- Chicken stock, 6 cup
- Ground cumin, 2 tsp.
- Ground coriander, 1 tsp.
- Black pepper
- Chopped squash, 2 cup
- Chopped cilantro, 1 tbsp.
- Cooked and shredded turkey meat, 4 cup
- Salt
- Garlic powder, ½ tsp.
- Salsa verde, ½ cup
- Chopped and canned chipotle peppers, 1 tbsp.

Directions:

1. Set up a pan on fire with stock over medium heat.
2. Mix in squash to cook for 10 minutes stirring gently.
3. Stir in chipotles, salsa verde, coriander, cumin, turkey and seasonings to cook for 10 minutes.
4. Mix in sour cream and remove from heat.
5. Set the mixture into bowls topped with chopped cilantro and serve.
6. Enjoy.

Nutrition:

Calories: 154, Fat: 5, Fiber: 3, Carbs: 2, Protein: 27

Keto Flax seed Chicken

Total time: 1 hour 10 minutes

Servings: 12

Ingredients:

- Provolone cheese, 8 oz.
- Keto pizza crust, 1.
- Onion powder, 1 tsp.
- Ground flax seed, ¼ cup
- Black pepper
- Grated parmesan, ½ cup
- De-boned and sliced chicken breasts, 1 lb.
- Keto marinara sauce, ½ cup
- Eggs, 2.
- Salt
- Italian seasoning, 1 tsp.
- Garlic powder, 1 tsp.

Directions:

1. Set a mixing bowl in position to combine garlic powder, Italian seasoning with onion, flax seed, salt, parmesan, and pepper.
2. Set another medium bowl in place to whisk together eggs with seasonings
3. Pass the chicken pieces in eggs and then in seasoning mi.
4. Set the coated chicken pieces on a lined baking sheet.
5. Set the oven for 30 minutes at 350°F, allow to bake
6. Set the pizza crust dough on a lined baking sheet and top half of the provolone cheese on half
7. Remove the chicken from the oven the chop and spread over provolone cheese
8. Top the marinara sauce and then the remaining cheese
9. Cover all these with the other half of the dough and shape your cal zone and seal the edges
10. Set the oven at 350°F, allow to bake for 20 minutes
11. Allow cooling before slicing to serve.

Nutrition:

Calories: 340, Fat: 8, Fiber: 2, Carbs: 6, Protein: 20

Pecan Crusted Chicken

Total time: 30 minutes

Servings: 4

Ingredients:

- Whisked egg, 1.
- Salt
- Chopped pecans, 1½ cups.
- Chicken breasts, 4.
- Black pepper
- Coconut oil, 3 tbsps.

Directions:

1. Set the whisked egg in a bowl then pecans in another one
2. Rub the chicken with some seasonings then pass in egg then in the pecans to coat evenly
3. Set the pan on fire with oil to brown the chicken pieces on both sides
4. Set the chicken in a baking tray.
5. Set the oven at 350ºF allow to bake for 10 minutes
6. Set on plates to serve.
7. Enjoy.

Nutrition:

Calories: 320, Fat: 12, Fiber: 4, Carbs: 1, Protein: 30

Chapter4 Dinner

Chicken and Mustard Sauce

The preparation and cooking time is 40 minutes and can sufficiently serve 3 people

Ingredients:

- Sweet Paprika – ¼tsp.
- Chopped Bacon Strips – 8
- Dijon Mustard – 1/3 cup
- Salt and Pepper
- Chicken Stocks – 1½ cups
- Chopped yellow onion – 1 cup
- Chicken Stock – 1½ cup
- Olive Oil – 1 tablespoon

Directions:

1. Get a bowl and add up, Paprika with mustard, pepper, salt, mix until it's evenly combined
2. Spread the mixture on the chicken breast and massage
3. Get a pan over a medium heat
4. Add the Bacon, stir and cook until it gets brown, and you can later transfer it to the plate
5. Heat the pan one more time and prepare for some time
6. Put the salt, pepper, Bacon and onions and stir thoroughly
7. Put back the chicken to the pan, and cook over medium heat for 20 minutes, turn the meat halfway
8. Share the chicken on plates, drizzle the source over it and serve

Nutrition:

Fat 8, Protein 26, Calories 223, Carbs 3, Fiber 1

Easy Italian Chicken Recipe

The preparation and cooking time is 1 hour 10 minutes a can sufficiently serve 6 people

Ingredients:

- Chicken Stock – ½ cup
- Chopped cherry peppers – 6
- Dried Oregano – 2tsp.
- Salt and black pepper
- Minced garlic – 2 tablespoons
- Chopped Italian Sausage – 1 pound
- Salt and pepper

- Chopped bell pepper – 1
- Halved Cherry Tomatoes – 2 Cups
- Balsamic Vinegar – 1 tablespoon
- Chopped Parsley
- Chopped mushrooms – 8
- Italian Sausage – 1 pound
- Dried Oregano – 2tsp.

Directions:

1. Add salt and pepper and rub the chicken with half of the Oil
2. Preheat a pan for 2 minutes over high temperature
3. Place the chicken over high heat, flip and cook for 2 minutes
4. Introduce the chicken into an oven at 450 °F and get it baked for 8 minutes
5. Bring out the chicken out of the table and divide between plates
6. Heat the rest of the Oil over medium heat, add the necessaries such as the chill flakes, onion, garlic, olives, capers, anchovies
7. Stir thoroughly and cook for 1 minute
8. Put the salt, tomatoes and pepper, stir and cook for 2 minutes
9. Drizzle over chicken breast and serve

Nutrition:

Calories 400, Protein 7, Fat 20, Carbs 20

Tasty Caesar Salad

Total Time: 10 minutes

Serves: 2

Ingredients:

- Creamy Caesar dressing, 3 tbsps.
- Pitted and sliced avocado, 1.
- Salt.
- Cooked and crumbled bacon, 1 cup
- Grilled and shredded chicken breast, 1.
- Black pepper.

Directions:

1. Combine avocado with chicken breast and bacon in a salad bowl.
2. Mix in the seasonings and Caesar dressing to coat evenly
3. Set into 2 bowls and serve

Nutrition:

Calories: 334, fat: 23, fiber: 4, carbs: 3, protein: 18

Meatballs and Tzatziki salad

Preparation and cooking time: 25 minutes

Serves: 6

Ingredients:

- Ground beef- 17 oz.
- Jarred tzatziki- 7 oz.
- Cherry tomatoes: halved- 7 oz.
- Dried oregano- 2 ½ tsp.
- Almond milk- ¼ cup
- Chopped mint- ¼ cup
- Grated yellow onion- 1
- Minced garlic cloves- 2
- Bread slices: torn- 5
- Chopped parsley- ¼ cup
- Whisked egg- 1
- Lemon juice- 1½ tbsp.
- Thinly sliced cucumber- 1
- Baby spinach- 1 cup
- Salt
- Black pepper

Directions

1. Soak torn bread in milk in a bowl for 3 minutes. Remove the bread, squeeze the milk and chop it.
2. In a bowl, add the bread, beef, oregano, mint, salt, pepper, onion, parsley and garlic together and shape into balls.
3. Pour half of the oil into a pan over medium heat and sear meatballs all around for 8 minutes.
4. Remove and set aside.
5. Mix cucumber, tomato, and spinach in a salad bowl and add the remaining oil, salt, pepper, tzatziki, meatballs, and lemon juice.
6. Toss and serve.

Nutrition:

Calories 200, carbs 3, protein 7, fiber 1, fat 4

Slow cook spicy beef roast

Preparation and cooking time: 8 hours 10 minutes

Serves: 8

Ingredients:

- Beef roast- 5 Ib.
- Pinch of cayenne pepper
- Garlic powder- ½ tsp.
- Sweet paprika- 1 tbsp.
- Beef stock- ½ cup
- Minced garlic- 1 tbsp.
- Dry mustard- ¼ tsp.
- Avocado oil- 1 tbsp.
- Celery salt- ½ tsp.
- Chili powder- 2 tsp.
- Salt and black pepper

Directions

1. Brown beef on a pan with oil over medium-high on all sides.
2. Mix chili, celery salt, paprika, cayenne, garlic powder, salt, pepper and mustard powder in a bowl.
3. Add the roast beef to the spice mix and rub generously.
4. Put it in the slow cooker with beef stock and garlic and cook for 8 hours on low.
5. Slice beef and let cool.
6. Serve drizzled with strained juices.

Nutrition:

Calories 180, carbs 5, protein 25, fiber 1, fat 5

Baked meatballs and sauce

Preparation and cooking time: 35 minutes

Serves: 6

Ingredients:

- Ground beef- 2 Ib.
- Almond flour- ¾ cup
- Coconut aminos- 1 tbsp.
- Beef stock- ¼ cup
- Garlic powder- ½ tsp.
- Onion flakes- 1 tbsp.
- Chopped parsley- 1 tbsp.
- Salt and pepper

Sauce:

- Chopped yellow onion- 1 cup
- Ghee- 2 tbsp.
- Sliced mushrooms- 2 cups
- Bacon fat- 2 tbsp.
- Coconut aminos- ½ tsp.
- Beef stock- ½ cup
- Sour cream- ¼ cup
- Salt and pepper

Directions:

1. Combine beef with garlic powder, coconut aminos, almond flour, beef stock, parsley, salt and pepper and mold into beef balls.
2. Place them on a baking sheet and bake for 18 minutes at 375°F.
3. Dissolve the ghee and bacon fat on a pan over medium heat and mix in the mushrooms and let it cook for 4 minutes.
4. Mix in the onions and let it cook for 4 minutes.
5. Pour beef stock into the pan and add coconut aminos and sour cream.
6. Remove from heat and season with pepper and salt.
7. Serve drizzled with mushroom sauce.

Nutrition:

Calories 435, carbs 6, protein 32, fiber 4, fat 23

Grilled lamb with salad

Preparation and cooking time: 45 minutes

Serves: 4

Ingredients:

- Pinch of dried thyme
- Leg of lamb: bone removed and butterflied – 3 Ib.
- Ground cumin- 1 tsp.
- Minced garlic- 2 cloves
- Olive oil- 1 tbsp.
- Salt and pepper

Salad

- Chopped mint- 1 cup
- Spinach- 2 cups
- Crumbled feta cheese- 4 oz.
- Pecans- ½ cup
- Olive oil- ¼ cup
- Lemon juice- 1½ tbsp.

Directions

1. Coat the lamb with a mix of 1 tbsp. of oil, garlic, cumin, thyme, salt and pepper.
2. Grill on medium-high for 40 minutes.
3. Bake pecan on a lined baking sheet for 10 minutes at 350°F.
4. Let it cool and then slice.
5. Mix feta cheese, mint, spinach, lemon juice, olive oil, salt and pepper together
6. Serve sliced lamb on a bed of vegetables.

Nutrition:

Calories 334, carbs 5, protein 7, fiber 3, fat 33

Simple Baked Turkey Recipe

The preparation and cooking time is 55 minutes and can sufficiently serve 8 people

Ingredients:

- Poultry seasoning – 1tsp.
- Grated Cheese Parmesan – ½ cup
- Zucchinis – 4 cups (cut with a spiralizer)
- Cream cheese – ½ cup
- Shredded cup cabbage – 3 cups
- Turkey stock – ½ cup
- Cooked and shredded turkey meat – 3 cups
- Whisked egg – 1
- Garlic powder – ¼tsp. shredded cabbage – 3 cups
- Salt and pepper
- Cup turkey stock

Directions:

1. Put stock in a pan and place under medium heat
2. Put the cream, cheddar cheese, Parmesan, pepper, poultry seasoning, garlic powder, egg and stir to bring low cooking
3. Put the turkey meat and cabbage, stir thoroughly and take off heat
4. Add the Zucchini noodles in a baking dish, and add some salt, pepper, and turkey mix and spread
5. Cover with tin foil and introduce to 400 ºF, and bake for 35 minutes
6. Leave aside to cool down before serving

Nutrition:

Calories240, Fiber 1, Protein 25, Fat 15

Walnut-Cranberry Turkey Salad

The preparation and cooking time is 10 minutes and can sufficiently serve 4 people

Ingredients

- Orange Juice – 1 cup
- Cranberries – ¼ cup
- Chopped Walnuts – 3 tablespoons
- Peeled and cut to small segments – 1 Orange
- Cored and chopped red Apple – 1

- Cooked and cubed turkey breast – 2 cups
- Peeled and sliced Kiwis – 3
- Orange juice – 1 cup
- Torn romaine lettuce leaves – 4 cups

Directions:

1. Get a salad bowl, mix up the lettuce, with orange segments, turkey, apples, walnut and cranberries
2. In a separate bowl, mix cranberry sauce with the orange juice and stir
3. Drizzle over the turkey salad, toss to coat and serve with kiwis on top

Nutrition:

Calories 120, Fiber 1, Protein 7, Carbs 3

Spinach Artichoke Stuffed Chicken Breast

The preparation and cooking time is 60 minutes and can sufficiently serve 4 people

Ingredients:

- Dried onions – 1 tablespoon
- Shredded Mozzarella – 4 ounces
- Dried garlic – 1 tablespoon
- Grated Parmesan – ½ cup
- Salt and pepper
- Cream cheese – 4 ounces
- Spinach – 10 ounces
- Chopped canned artichoke hearts – 10 ounces
- Chicken breast – 4

Directions:

1. Arrange the chicken breast on a lined baking sheet
2. Add salt and pepper and introduce to an oven at 400 degrees and bake for 30 minutes
3. Get a bowl, mix up the cream cheese, Parmesan, spinach, salt, garlic, pepper and stir
4. Bring the chicken out of the oven, cut each piece in the middle, divide the artichoke mix and add some mozzarella
5. Place in the oven at 400 °F, and bake for 15 minutes

Nutrition:

Calories 450, Carbs 3, Protein 39, Fat 23, Fiber 1

Keto Chicken Thighs

The preparation and cooking time is 55 minutes and can sufficiently serve 4 people

Ingredients:

- Skin and bone-in chicken thighs – 6
- Sliced mushrooms – 8 ounces
- Salt and black pepper
- Minced garlic cloves – 2
- Grated Gruyere cheese – 2 tablespoon
- Ghee – 3 tablespoon

Directions:

1. Put a tablespoon of ghee in a pan and place over medium heat
2. Add the chicken thighs
3. Put the salt and pepper and cook for 1 minute
4. Heat the pan again the rest of the ghee, add garlic, stir thoroughly and cook for 1 minute
5. Put the mushroom and stir well
6. Put salt and pepper, stir and cook for 10 minutes
7. Spoon these over chicken, sprinkle Cheese and introduce to the oven at 350 °F and bake for 30 minutes
8. Switch the oven to broiler and broil everything for a couple of minutes
9. Share it within plates and serve.

Nutrition:

Protein 64, Calories 340,Fat 31Carbs 5, Fiber 3

Tasty Turkey Pie Recipe

The preparation and cooking time is 50 minutes and can sufficiently serve 6 people

Ingredients:

- Cooked and shredded turkey meat
- Paprika – ¼tsp.
- Garlic powder – ¼tsp.
- Chopped thyme – 1tsp.
- Chopped kale – ½ cup
- Turkey stock – 2 cups
- Shredded Cheddar Cheese – ½ cup
- Peeled, chopped, butternut squash – ½ cup
- Salt and black pepper
- Cooking spray
- Xanthan gum – ½tsp.

For the crust

- Ghee – ¼ cup
- Almond flour – 2 cups
- Salt – A pinch
- Egg – 1
- Xanthan gum – ¼tsp.
- Cheddar Cheese – ¼ cup

Directions:

1. Put stock in a pot and place it over medium heat
2. Put the turkey meat and squash, stir thoroughly and simmer for 10 minutes
3. Add the thyme, Paprika, salt, pepper, powder and garlic
4. Add cheddar cheese and stir well. Place it off the heat
5. In a separate bowl, mix in ½ cup stock from the pot and ¼tsp. xanthan gum, stir thoroughly
6. Add egg, ghee and cheddar cheese
7. Stir continuously until you attain your desired pie crust dough
8. Shape a ball and carefully place in the fridge
9. Spray cooking spray on a baking dish and spread pie filling on the bottom
10. Arrange the dough to a working surface, roll into a circle and top filling with this

11. Press and neaten the edges
12. Place in an oven at 350 ºF and bake for 35 minutes
13. Bring it out, allow it to cool and serve

Nutrition:

Fiber 8, Protein 16, Calories 320, Fat 23, Carbs 6

Lemon Trout And Ghee Sauce

Total time: 20 minutes

Servings: 4

Ingredients:

- Chopped chives, 3 tbsps.
- Trout fillets, 4.
- Salt
- Olive oil, 2 tbsps.
- Grated lemon zest, 3 tsp.
- Black pepper
- Lemon juice, 2 tsp.
- Ghee, 6 tbsps.

Directions:

1. Rub the trout with the seasonings and olive oil
2. Heat up the kitchen grill over medium heat to cook the fish fillets for four minutes both sides.
3. In the meantime, set the pan on fire with ghee to cook chives, pepper, salt, lemon juice and zest
4. Set the fish fillets on plate served with the ghee sauce.
5. Enjoy.

Nutrition:

Calories: 320, Fat: 12, Fiber: 1, Carbs: 2, Protein: 24

Creamy Clam Chowder

Total time: 2 hours 10 minutes

Servings: 4

Ingredients:

- Chicken stock, 2 cup
- Salt
- Chopped bacon slices, 13.
- Chopped celery stalks, 1 cup
- Ground thyme, 1 tsp.
- Whipping cream, 2 cup
- Canned baby clams, 14 oz.
- Black pepper.
- Chopped onion, 1 cup

Directions:

1. Set a pan on fire to brown the bacon slices over medium heat then set on the bowl.
2. Set the same pan on fire over medium heat to cook the celery for five minutes.
3. Set everything in the Crockpot with stock, whipping cream, thyme, seasonings, baby clams and stir.
4. Cook on for 2 hours high.
5. Set into bowls and serve.
6. Enjoy.

Nutrition:

Calories: 420, Fat: 22, Fiber: 0, Carbs: 5, Protein: 25

Barramundi with Cherry tomatoes

Total time: 22 minutes

Servings: 4

Ingredients:

- Barramundi fillets, 2.
- Chopped black olives, ¼ cup
- Chopped parsley, 2 tbsps.
- Olive oil, 2 tsp.
- Lemon zest, 1 tbsp.
- Italian seasoning, 2 tsp.
- Salt
- Chopped cherry tomatoes, ¼ cup
- Olive oil, 1 tbsp.
- Black pepper
- Chopped green olives, ¼ cup
- Lemon zest, 2 tbsps.

Directions:

1. Season the fish with Italian seasoning, salt, 2tsps. olive oil and pepper.
2. Set on a baking tray and reserve.
3. In the meantime, combine tomatoes with all the olives, 1 tablespoon oil, lemon zest, salt, pepper, lemon zest, and parsley in a bowl evenly.
4. Set the oven for 12 minutes at 400 °F allow to bake
5. Serve on plates topped with tomato relish.

Nutrition:

Calories: 150, Fat: 4, Fiber: 2, Carbs: 1, Protein: 10

Fried Shrimp

Total time: 20 minutes

Servings: 4

Ingredients:

- Deveined shrimp, 1 lb.
- Black pepper.
- Ghee, 1 tbsp.
- Lemon zest, 1 tbsp.
- Olive oil, 2 tbsps.
- Salt.
- Lemon juice, 2 tbsps.
- Minced garlic, 2 tbsps.

Directions:

1. Set the pan on fire to melt the ghee and oil for cooking the shrimp for 2minutes
2. Gently stir in the garlic to cook for 4 minutes
3. Mix in salt, lemon juice, pepper, and lemon zest
4. Remove from heat to serve immediately

Nutrition:

Calories: 149, Fat: 1, Fiber: 3, Carbs: 1, Protein: 6

Baked Calamari And Shrimp Drizzled With Sauce and Lemon Juice

Prep + Cook Time: 30 minutes
Servings: 1
Ingredients:

- Calamari; cut into medium rings - 8 ounces.
- Shrimp; peeled and deveined - 7 ounces.
- Egg - 1
- Tomato paste - 1tsp.
- Mayonnaise - 1 tablespoon.
- A splash of Worcestershire sauce.
- Lemon juice - 1tsp.
- Coconut flour - 3 tablespoons.
- Coconut oil - 1 tablespoon.
- Avocado; chopped - 2 tablespoons.
- Turmeric - ½tsp.
- Lemon slices - 2 lemons.
- Salt and black pepper to the taste.

Directions:

1. Gather a mixer bowl to whisk the egg with coconut oil together.

2. Toss the calamari rings and shrimps into the bowl to coat everything well.

3. Take another bowl and add flour with salt, pepper and turmeric and stir well together.

4. Spread out a lined baking sheet and dredge calamari and shrimps into the flour mix and place them evenly on the sheet.

5. Put this into the oven at 400 ºF and bake for 10 minutes.

6. Take out the baking sheet, flip calamari and shrimps and again bake for 10 minutes.

7. In the meantime, mix avocado with mayo and tomato paste in a bowl and with the help of a fork, mash all the ingredients together.

8. Stir well by adding Worcestershire sauce, lemon juice, salt and pepper into the avocado mix.
9. Assemble baked calamari and shrimps on separate plates and serve it with the sauce and lemon juice on the side.

Nutrition:

Calories: 368; Fat : 23; Fiber : 3; Carbs : 10; Protein : 34

Shrimp And Snow Peas Soup Recipe

Prep + Cook Time: 20 minutes
Servings: 4

Ingredients:

- Shrimp; peeled and deveined - 1 pound.
- Snow peas - ½ pound.
- Sesame oil - 1 tablespoon.
- Chili oil - ½ tablespoon.
- Scallions; chopped - 4
- Coconut oil - 1 ½ tablespoon.
- Small ginger root; finely chopped - 1
- Chicken stock - 8 cups.
- Coconut aminos - ¼ cup.
- Canned bamboo shoots; sliced - 5 ounces.
- Black pepper to the taste.
- Fish sauce - ¼tsp.

Directions:

1. Pour some oil in a pot and heat it up over medium heat.
2. Once the oil is warm, add scallions and ginger and stir for 2 minutes until it's cooked.
3. Put coconut aminos, stock, black pepper and fish sauce and give it a mix and bring it to a boil.
4. Now, add shrimp, snow peas and bamboo shoots and give it another stir and let it cook for another 3 minutes.
5. Drizzle some sesame oil and hot chilli oil. Give it a last one mix and serve hot in separate bowls.

Nutrition:

Calories: 200; Fat : 3; Fiber : 2; Carbs : 4; Protein : 14

Chapter5 Snack & Appetizer

Basil Pesto Crackers

Prep + Cook Time: 27 minutes

Servings: 6

Ingredients:

- Baking powder-1/2tsp. r
- Basil, a dried-1/4tsp.
- Almond flour-1¼ cups
- Garlic clove, minced-1
- Basil pesto-2 tablespoons
- Cayenne pepper- a pinch
- Ghee-3 tablespoons
- Salt and black pepper - to the taste

Directions:

1. Whisk almond flour with salt, pepper and baking powder.
2. Stir in basil, garlic, pesto, and cayenne
3. Mix well then add ghee. Stir well to form a smooth dough.
4. Spread this dough in a baking sheet lined with wax paper.
5. Bake the crust for 17 minutes at 325 ᵒF
6. Allow the crust to cool then break it into small crackers.
7. Enjoy.

Nutrition:

Calories: 200; Fat: 20g; Fiber: 1g; Carbs: 4g; Protein: 7g

Pepperoni Pizza Dip

Prep + Cook Time: 30 minutes

Servings: 4

Ingredients:

- Cream cheese, soft-4 ounces
- Tomato sauce-1/2 cup
- Mayonnaise -1/4 cup
- Mozzarella cheese-1/2 cup
- Pepperoni slices, chopped-6
- Italian seasoning -1/2tsp.
- Sour cream -1/4 cup
- Parmesan cheese, grated - 1/4 cup
- Green bell pepper, a chopped-1 tablespoon
- Black olives pitted and chopped-4
- Salt and black pepper - to the taste

Directions:

1. Whisk cream cheese, mayo, mozzarella, salt, pepper and sour cream in a suitable bowl.
2. Divide this mixture into 4 ramekins and top it with tomato sauce.
3. Add parmesan cheese, pepperoni, bell pepper, black olives and Italian seasoning on top.
4. Bake the ramekins for 20 minutes at 350 °F.
5. Enjoy right away.

Nutrition:

Calories: 400; Fat: 34g; Fiber: 4g; Carbs: 4g; Protein: 15g

Spinach Fat Bombs

Prep + Cook Time: 22 minutes

Servings: 30

Ingredients:

- Melted ghee -4 tablespoons
- Eggs-2
- Almond flour -1 cup
- Spinach-16 ounces
- Feta cheese, crumbled -1/3 cup
- Nutmeg, ground -1/4tsp.
- Parmesan, grated -1/3 cup
- Onion powder -1 tablespoon
- Whipping cream-3 tablespoons
- Garlic powder -1tsp.
- Salt and black pepper - to the taste

Directions:

1. Blend spinach with eggs, ghee, feta cheese, nutmeg, parmesan, almond flour, salt, pepper cream, garlic pepper, and onion until smooth.
2. Freeze this mixture for 10 minutes then makes 30 balls out of this.
3. Place these balls in a baking sheet, lined with wax paper.
4. Bake these spinach balls for 12 minutes at 350 °F.
5. Allow them to cool then serve.

Nutrition:

Calories: 60; Fat: 5g; Fiber: 1g; Carbs: 0.7g; Protein: 2g

Jalapeno Bacon Bombs

Prep + Cook Time: 20 minutes

Servings: 3

Ingredients:

- Bacon slices -3
- Cream cheese- 3 ounces
- Parsley, a dried-1/2tsp.
- Garlic powder -1/4tsp.
- Onion powder-1/4tsp.
- Jalapeno pepper, chopped-1
- Salt and black pepper - to the taste

Directions:

1. Place a pan over medium-high heat.
2. Stir in bacon and sauté until crispy then transfer them to a plate lined with a paper towel.
3. Remove and reserve the bacon fat.
4. Whisk cream cheese, onion and garlic powder, salt, pepper, parsley and jalapeno pepper in a suitable bowl.
5. Stir in bacon fat and crumbled bacon.
6. Mix well and make small fat bombs out of it.
7. Enjoy.

Nutrition:

Calories: 200; Fat: 18g; Fiber: 1g; Carbs: 2g; Protein: 5g

Mini Zucchini Pizzas

Prep + Cook Time: 25 minutes

Servings: 4

Ingredients:

- Mozzarella, shredded-1 cup
- Zucchini, sliced-1
- Tomato sauce-1/4 cup
- Cumin - a pinch
- Cooking spray
- Salt and black pepper - to the taste

Directions:

1. Grease a baking sheet with cooking spray.
2. Place Zucchini slices in the baking sheet in a single layer.
3. Top each slice with tomato sauce, salt, pepper, cumin, and mozzarella.
4. Bake these slices for 15 minutes at 350 ºF.
5. Devour.

Nutrition:

Calories: 140; Fat: 4g; Fiber: 2g; Carbs: 6g; Protein: 4g

Zucchini Tahini Hummus

Prep + Cook Time: 10 minutes

Servings: 5

Ingredients:

- Zucchinis, finely chopped- 4 cups
- Olive oil-1/4 cup
- Garlic cloves, minced -4
- Tahini-¾ cup
- Lemon juice -1/2 cup
- Cumin, ground -1 tablespoon
- Salt and black pepper - to the taste

Directions:

1. Add zucchinis, lemon juice, tahini, cumin, garlic, oil, salt, and black pepper to a blender.
2. Pulse well until it forms a smooth mixture.
3. Enjoy.

Nutrition:

Calories: 80; Fat: 5g; Fiber: 3g; Carbs: 6g; Protein: 7g

Amber Beef Jerky

Prep + Cook Time: 10 hours

Servings: 6

Ingredients:

- Beef round, sliced -2 pounds
- Amber -24 ounces
- Black peppercorns -2 tablespoons
- Black pepper -2 tablespoons
- Soy sauce -2 cups
- Worcestershire sauce -1/2 cup

Directions:

1. Whisk soy sauce with black pepper, Worcestershire sauce and black peppercorns in a suitable bowl.
2. Place the beef slices in the peppercorn bowl and mix well to coat.
3. Marinate for 6 hours in the refrigerator.
4. Place these marinated slices on a rack of the oven.
5. Bake them for 4 hours at 370 ºF.
6. Devour.

Nutrition:

Calories: 300; Fat: 12g; Fiber: 4g; Carbs: 3g; Protein: 8g

Crab Mayonnaise Dip

Prep + Cook Time: 40 minutes

Servings: 8

Ingredients:

- Bacon strips, sliced -8
- Crab meat -12 ounces
- Mayonnaise -1/2 cup
- Sour cream -1/2 cup
- Garlic cloves, minced -4
- Green onions, minced -4
- Cream cheese -8 ounces
- Poblano pepper, chopped -2
- Lemon juice -2 tablespoons
- Parmesan cheese, grated -1 cup
- Salt and black pepper - to the taste

Directions:

1. Place a pan over medium-high heat.
2. Stir in bacon and sauté until crispy then transfer to a plate lined with a paper towel.
3. Chop the cooked bacon and keep it aside.
4. Whisk cream cheese with mayo, bacon, green onion, poblano peppers, lemon juice and parmesan in a suitable bowl.
5. Stir in crabmeat, black pepper, and salt. Mix well gently.
6. Add this mixture to a greased baking dish then bake for 20 minutes at 350 °F.
7. Enjoy with a cucumber stick and a dip

Nutrition:

Calories: 200; Fat: 7g; Fiber: 2g; Carbs: 4g; Protein: 6g

Chapter6 Dessert

Easy Butter Delight

Prep + Cook Time: 14 minutes

Servings: 16

Ingredients:

- vanilla extract-1/2tsp.
- coconut butter-4 ounces
- sugar-free dark chocolate; - 4 ounces
- cocoa butter-4 ounces
- xanthan gum-1/8tsp.
- swerve-1/4 cup
- peanut butter-1/2 cup

Directions:

1. Start by putting all the butter and swerve in a pan and heat up over medium heat until they melt.
2. Mix with xanthan gum and vanilla extract and Stir until they all combine.
3. Stir well again, pour into a lined baking sheet and spread well. refrigerate for 10 minutes
4. Put water in a pan and heat to over medium-high heat and bring to a simmer.
5. Add a bowl on top of the pan and add chocolate to the bowl.
6. Stir until it melts and trickle over butter mix.
7. refrigerate until everything is firm, cut into 16 pieces and serve

Nutrition:

Calories: 176; Fiber : 2; Protein : 3; Carbs : 5; Fat : 15;

Homemade Coconut Pudding

Prep + Cook Time: 20 minutes

Servings: 4

Ingredients:

- 1/2tsp. vanilla extract
- coconut milk-1 2/3 cups
- gelatin-1 tablespoon
- egg yolks-3
- swerve-6 tablespoons

Directions:

1. Start by mixing gelatin with 1 tablespoon coconut milk In a bowl; stir well and set aside for now.
2. Put the rest of the milk into a pan and heat up over medium heat.
3. Include swerve; stir and cook for 7 minutes
4. mix egg yolks with the hot coconut milk and vanilla extract in a bowl stir well and return the mix to the pan.
5. Cook mix for 4 minutes then include gelatin and stir properly.
6. Divide this into 4 ramekins and refrigerate pudding for 3 hours
7. Serve cold.

Nutrition:

Calories: 140; Fiber : 0; Fat : 2; Carbs : 2; Protein : 2

Easy Delicious Mousse

Prep + Cook Time: 10 minutes

Serves: 12

Ingredients:

- mascarpone cheese-8 ounces
- blueberries-1/2 pint
- strawberries-1/2 pint
- whipping cream-1 cup
- vanilla stevia-¾tsp.

Directions:

1. Put the whipping cream with stevia and mascarpone in a bowl; mix and blend well using your mixer.
2. Place a layer of blueberries and strawberries in 12 glasses, then a layer of cream and so on.
3. Serve cold

Nutrition:

Calories: 143; Fiber : 1; Protein : 2; Carbs : 3; Fat : 12;

Mint Delight

Prep + Cook Time: 2 hours 10 minutes

Serves: 3

Ingredients:

- melted coconut oil-1/2 cup
- cocoa powder-1 tablespoon
- stevia drops-3

For the pudding:

- pitted, peeled and chopped avocado-1
- canned coconut milk-14 ounces
- peppermint oil-1tsp.
- Drops stevia-10

Directions:

1. mix coconut oil with cocoa powder in a bowl and 3 drops stevia; stir well
2. Transfer the mix to a lined container and refrigerate for 1 hour.
3. Dice this into small pieces and set aside for now.
4. Mix coconut milk with avocado, 10 drops stevia and peppermint oil in your blender and pulse well.
5. Add chocolate chips, fold them gently
6. Divide the pudding into bowls and keep in the fridge for 1 more hour.

Nutrition:

Calories: 140; Fiber : 2; Carbs : 3; Fat : 3; Protein : 4

Sugar-Free Keto Cheesecakes

Prep + Cook Time: 25 minutes

Serves: 9

Ingredients:

For the cheesecakes:

- sugar-free caramel syrup-1 tablespoon
- butter-2 tablespoons
- coffee-3 tablespoons
- swerve-1/3 cup
- cream cheese-8 ounces
- eggs-3

For the frosting:

- soft mascarpone cheese-8 ounces
- swerve-2 tablespoons
- caramel syrup; sugar free-3 tablespoons
- butter-3 tablespoons

Directions:

1. Put the cream cheese with eggs, butter, coffee, caramel syrup and swerve in your blender and blend very well.
2. Spoon this into a cupcakes pan
3. Preheat oven to about 350 °F and introduce the cupcake pan and bake for 15 minutes
4. Set the cupcakes aside to cool down and then keep in the freezer for about 3 hours
5. On the other hand; in a new bowl, mix them with caramel syrup, swerve and mascarpone cheese and blend till smooth.
6. Spoon this over cheesecakes and serve them.

Nutrition: Calories: 254; Fiber : 0; Carbs : 1; Protein : 5; Fat : 23

Delicious Chocolate Pie

Prep + Cook Time: 30 minutes
Serves: 10
Ingredients:
For the crust:

- Butter-3 tablespoons
- butter for the pan-1tsp.
- baking powder-1/2tsp.
- vanilla extract-1½tsps.
- almond crust-1½ cup
- stevia-1/3 cup
- salt- A pinch
- egg-1

For the filling:

- vanilla extract-1 tablespoon
- butter-4 tablespoons
- sour cream-4 tablespoons
- granulated stevia
- 1 cup whipping cream
- 16 ounces cream cheese
- 1/2 cup cut stevia
- 1/2 cup cocoa powder
- 1tsp. vanilla extract

Directions:

1. Pick your spring form pan and grease with 1tsp. butter and set aside for a while.
2. Mix the baking powder in a bowl with stevia, a pinch of salt and almond flour and stir till even.
3. Include butter, egg and vanilla extract; stir until you obtain a smooth dough.
4. Press this mix well into the springform pan
5. Introduce this into the oven at 375 °F and bake for 11 minutes
6. Remove the pie crust out of the oven then cover with tin foil and bake for 8 minutes more
7. Take the pie crust out again of the oven and set it aside to cool down.

8. Get a bowl and mix your cream cheese with butter, sour cream, vanilla extract, cocoa powder and stevia and stir properly.
9. In another bowl, use your mixer to mix whipping cream with stevia and vanilla extract and stir using your mixer.
10. Combine the 2 mixtures and pour into pie crust
11. Spread well, refrigerate for 3 hours and then serve cold.

Nutrition: Calories: 450; Fiber : 3; Carbs : 7; Protein : 7; Fat : 43.

Vanilla Keto Sugar-Free Ice Cream

Prep + Cook Time: 3 hours 10 minutes
Servings: 6
Ingredients:

- eggs; yolks and whites separated-4
- swerve-1/2 cup
- heavy whipping cream-1¼ cup
- vanilla extract-1 tablespoon
- cream of tartar-1/4tsp.

Directions:
1. Mix egg whites with cream of tartar and swerve in a bowl; stir using your mixer.
2. Meanwhile, in a new bowl whisk cream with vanilla extract and blend properly.
3. Properly combine the 2 mixtures and stir gently.
4. In another bowl, whisk egg yolks very well and then add the two egg whites mix.
5. Stir gently, pour this into a container
6. Keep in the freezer for 3 hours before serving your ice cream.

Nutrition: Calories: 243Fiber : 0; Carbs : 2; Protein : 4; ; Fat : 22;

Chapter7 28-Day Meal Plan

Meal Plan	Breakfast	Lunch	Dinner	Side Dish & Snack
Day 1	Sausage and Asparagus and Egg Baked Breakfast	Chicken & Garnished Shrimp	Chicken and Mustard Sauce	Basil Pesto Crackers
Day 2	Parsley Biscuits	Zucchini Noodles and Bacon Salad	Easy Italian Chicken Recipe	Easy Butter Delight
Day 3	Tomato and Serrano Pepper Shakshouka	Pan-Fried Crab Cakes	Tasty Caesar Salad	Pepperoni Pizza Dip
Day 4	Bacon and Lemon Thyme Muffins	Spicy beef sauerkraut soup bowls	Meatballs and Tzatziki salad	Homemade Coconut Pudding
Day 5	Bacon and Avocado Muffins	Spicy beef soup	Slow cook spicy beef roast	Spinach Fat Bombs
Day 6	Radish and Corned Beef Hash	Easy Turkey and Tomato Curry	Baked meatballs and sauce	Easy Delicious Mousse
Day 7	Soft Cinnamon Pancakes	Creamy Mushroom Chicken Recipe	Grilled lamb with salad	Jalapeno Bacon Bombs
Day8	Flax, Chia, and Pumpkin Pancakes	Chicken Breast with Olive Tapenade	Simple Baked Turkey Recipe	Mint Delight
Day9	Brussels Sprouts with Eggs and Bacon	Stuffed Chicken Breast Recipe	Walnut-Cranberry Turkey Salad	Mini Zucchini Pizzas

Day10	Hemp, Flax and Chia Seeds Porridge	Mustard Salmon Meatballs	Spinach Artichoke Stuffed Chicken Breast	Sugar-Free Keto Cheesecakes
Day11	Tea Flavored Eggs	Pan-Fried Tuna Cakes	Keto Chicken Thighs	Zucchini Tahini Hummus
Day12	Beef, Olives, Avocado and Egg Breakfast Bowl	Tasty Salmon With Caper Sauce	Tasty Turkey Pie Recipe	Delicious Chocolate Pie
Day13	Creamy Feta Cheese Omelet	Tasty and Creamy Asparagus	Lemon Trout And Ghee Sauce	Amber Beef Jerky
Day14	Chia and Coconut Pudding	Seasoned Sprouts Salad	Creamy Clam Chowder	Vanilla Keto Sugar-Free Ice Cream
Day15	Sausage and Asparagus and Egg Baked Breakfast	Avocado Salad with Cilantro	Barramundi with Cherry tomatoes	Crab Mayonnaise Dip
Day16	Parsley Biscuits	Zucchini Cream with Parmesan	Fried Shrimp	Easy Butter Delight
Day17	Tomato and Serrano Pepper Shakshouka	Arugula And Hot Broccoli Soup	Baked Calamari And Shrimp Drizzled With Sauce and Lemon Juice	Basil Pesto Crackers
Day18	Bacon and Lemon Thyme Muffins	Spiced Turkey Chili	Shrimp And Snow Peas Soup Recipe	Homemade Coconut Pudding
Day19	Bacon and Avocado Muffins	Keto Flax seed Chicken	Chicken and Mustard Sauce	Pepperoni Pizza Dip

Day20	Radish and Corned Beef Hash	Pecan Crusted Chicken	Tasty Caesar Salad	Easy Delicious Mousse
Day21	Soft Cinnamon Pancakes	Zucchini Noodles and Bacon Salad	Slow cook spicy beef roast	Spinach Fat Bombs
Day22	Chia and Coconut Pudding	Spicy beef sauerkraut soup bowls	Grilled lamb with salad	Mint Delight
Day23	Creamy Feta Cheese Omelet	Easy Turkey and Tomato Curry	Walnut-Cranberry Turkey Salad	Jalapeno Bacon Bombs
Day24	Beef, Olives, Avocado and Egg Breakfast Bowl	Chicken Breast with Olive Tapenade	Keto Chicken Thighs	Sugar-Free Keto Cheesecakes
Day25	Tea Flavored Eggs	Mustard Salmon Meatballs	Lemon Trout And Ghee Sauce	Mini Zucchini Pizzas
Day26	Hemp, Flax and Chia Seeds Porridge	Tasty Salmon With Caper Sauce	Barramundi with Cherry tomatoes	Delicious Chocolate Pie
Day27	Brussels Sprouts with Eggs and Bacon	Seasoned Sprouts Salad	Baked Calamari And Shrimp Drizzled With Sauce and Lemon Juice	Zucchini Tahini Hummus
Day28	Flax, Chia, and Pumpkin Pancakes	Avocado Salad with Cilantro	Easy Italian Chicken Recipe	Vanilla Keto Sugar-Free Ice Cream

24980270R00052

Printed in Great Britain
by Amazon